delicious
asian
seafood
recipes

Lee Geok Boi

Contains easy step-by-step versions of all your favourite seafood recipes—from Sweet and Sour Whole Fish to Barbequed Sambal Stingray, Prawn Spring Rolls and Chilli Crab.

PERIPLUS

Basic Asian Ingredients

Candlenuts are waxy, cream-coloured nuts similar in size to macadamia nuts, which make a good substitute. They are never eaten raw but are ground and cooked with other seasonings. Store candlenuts in a cool, dry place.

Dried red chillies

Finger-length chillies

Bird's-eye chillies

Chillies come in many shapes and sizes. Fresh green and red **finger-length chillies** are moderately hot. Tiny red, green or yellow-orange **chilli padi** are very hot. **Dried chillies** are usually cut into lengths and soaked in warm water to soften before use. **Chilli powder** is made from ground dried chillies.

Coconut cream is made by adding $1/2$ cup (125 ml) water to the grated flesh of one coconut, then squeezing and straining it to obtain the liquid. Coconut cream and coconut milk are widely sold canned and in packets. They come in varying consistencies, and you will need to adjust the thickness by adding water as needed.

Coriander is a pungent herb and spice plant that is essential in Southeast Asian cooking. **Coriander leaves**, also known as cilantro, are sold in small bunches with the roots still intact. They are used as a flavouring and a garnish. Small, round coriander seeds are slightly citrussy in fragrance and are used whole or ground in curry pastes or spice mixes.

Cornstarch or cornflour is a fine white powder used as a thickening agent. It does not add much fat or change the flavour of a dish.

Dried shrimp paste or *belachan* is a dense mixture of fermented ground shrimp that must be toasted before use—either wrapped in foil and dry-roasted in a pan over low heat or toasted over a gas flame. It is sold in dried blocks and ranges from light brown to black in colour. Shrimp paste should be slightly toasted to enhance its flavour before using.

Fermented bean paste (*tau cheo*) is a richly-flavoured seasoning. The beans are fermented and salted and sold in jars. They vary in colour from dark brown to light golden. The basic fermented bean paste contains only soybeans, water and salt. It is also possible to buy slightly sweetened versions or those with added chilli. The beans are usually mashed with the back of a spoon before use.

Galangal (*lengkuas*) is similar in appearance to ginger and a member of the same family. This aromatic root has a distinct flavour that is used in curries throughout Southeast Asia. Dried galangal lacks the fragrance of fresh galangal, so try to buy it fresh. It can be sliced and kept sealed in the freezer for several months.

Kaffir lime leaves are used in soups and curries of Malay or Nonya origin.

They are also thinly sliced and used as a garnish.

Lemongrass is a highly aromatic herb. The tough outer layers of the stem should be peeled away and only the pale, inner flesh of the thick lower portions are used.

Spring onions are also known as scallions or green onions. They have slender stalks with dark green leaves and white bases. They are sliced and sprinkled generously on soups and as a garnish.

Turmeric is a root similar to ginger but with a bright yellow flesh and a more pungent flavour. Turmeric has antiseptic and stringent qualities and stains everything permanently, so scrub your knife blade, hands and chopping board immediately after handling. Purchase fresh turmeric root as needed as the flavour fades after a few days.

Tamarind pulp is the fruit of the tamarind seed pod. It is sold dried in packets or jars and generally still has some seeds and pod fibers mixed in with the dried pulp. It is used as a souring agent in many dishes. To obtain **tamarind juice**, soak the pulp in warm water for 5 minutes, mash well and then strain and discard any seeds and fibers, retaining only the juice.

Soy sauce is indispensable to Chinese cuisine. It is fermented from soya beans and salt, used in marinades, stir-fry cooking, sauces and dips. Low-salt varieties are now available. It is worth spending a little extra to purchase a high-quality soy sauce, because its distinctive flavour permeates Chinese cuisine, and a poor quality soy sauce can ruin the taste of even the best-cooked dish. Both light and black soy sauces are used in the recipes in this book.

Light Soy Sauce   Black Soy Sauce

How to buy fresh seafood

Fish Check the eyes, they should be gleaming and bright rather than dull and opaque. With some types of fish there may be flecks of blood in the eyes—this is fine if the blood looks bright red and the rest of the eye is still shining. Lift the gill flaps and look at the gills. They should be a bright dark red rather than a brownish red. If it is a scaly fish, check the scales, which should be firmly attached and not loose. When fish is not fresh, the flesh becomes soft. Prod the fish with a finger to see if the flesh is firm. There should be some resistance and the flesh should not feel mushy.

Prawns Look for pink spots in the heads (when the spots turn dark the prawns are already going off). The heads should be firmly attached to the body and not hanging loose. The shells should also look shiny, bright and be properly attached. Squeeze a prawn lightly between finger and thumb. The flesh should feel firm, not soft and mushy.

Squid Fresh squid looks shiny and the skin is smooth and still attached firmly to the body. Stroke it to see if the skin feels gritty. Press the flesh to see if it is firm and resilient—it should not feel soft.

Crabs and lobsters Obviously live crabs or lobsters are fresh. However, it is harder to tell if crabs and lobsters are fresh by their appearance once they are dead. Spiny lobsters, slipper lobsters and blue flower crabs are not usually sold live. Go with the smell which should be pleasant and iodine-like. Black crabs should never be purchased dead if possible although crab claws alone are acceptable. Again go by the smell. Female crabs may be more expensive because of the possibility of roe. It is easy to distinguish between male and female crabs: the males have a pointed underflap while female crabs have a more rounded, almost semicircular flap. Once cooked, crabs can also be firm or mushy and this mushiness has nothing to do with freshness. Needless to say, the preference is for firmness. Here, knowing a reliable fishmonger pays dividends. Skilled fishmongers always know when their crabs are good but it is not so easy for the average shopper to tell by appearance.

Other shellfish Clams, mussels and cockles are usually sold live. If the open shellfish closes up when touched, the shellfish is alive. Closed shellfish may not be dead either but if many are open, this is a good sign.

How to clean fresh seafood

Fish To scale fish, use a fish-scaler which is a sort of a double-edged serrated knife (line the sink with a few sheets of old newspaper before you scale the fish!). Gut fish as soon as possible—they keep better. To gut a fish, lay it flat against the cutting board. Using a sharp knife, slit the stomach open and remove the guts and gills. Rub in coarse salt then rinse away the blood and salt. Fish with firm scales can be grilled or steamed with the scales on although the fish should be gutted first. The scales help to keep the fish juicy. Just before serving, the scales can be lifted off in one piece by inserting a knife under the scales at the tail then flipping the scales away towards the head.

Prawns Unless prawns are to be steamed, grilled or barbecued whole, only minimum cleaning is needed—trim off the pointed tips of the head and the whiskers. Prawns may be cooked with head, tail and shell intact or completely removed. They may also be cooked with the heads and tails kept on but the rest of the shell removed or with just the tail left on (prawns cooked with the shell and head on are more juicy than shelled ones). If shelled or partially shelled, remove the black intestinal tract that runs down the back of the prawn.

Crabs and lobsters There are several ways to kill crabs. One is to place them in the freezer for an hour. An old Chinese method is to stick a chopstick or an icepick between the crab's eyes. A third way is to dunk them briefly in boiling water. This is a good method if you plan to steam the crabs. If you are cooking the crabs in some other way, it is better not to precook the flesh. Once dead, the crabs should be brushed clean under a running tap. When the crabs are clean, lift off the underflap and the shell. Discard the spongy gills on either side of the crab and the inedible bits like the stomach which is in the middle of the crab. Do not discard the roe which is a bright orange or yellow colour. Scrub the inside shell clean if it looks dirty. The claws can be separated from the body of the crab depending on their size. But they should be cracked before cooking to make the flesh more accessible. To clean spiny or slipper lobsters, twist off the head. If lobsters are being fried rather than steamed, the thin underside shell should be removed to allow the seasonings to penetrate into the flesh. To remove this shell, insert a sharp knife through it and using a clean pair of pliers, twist off the plastic-like shell leaving the hard top shell. Slipper lobsters can be twisted out of the shell with the tails still attached. To make this easier to do, first snip the ligaments on either side of the lobster just above the tail.

Other shellfish Other shellfish can be purged of sand and dirt by soaking them in heavily salted water for several hours. Rinse or scrub them before cooking. To clean mussels, pull off the beard and scrub them.

Sambal Lengkong (Spicy Fish Flakes)

1 kg (2 lbs) mackerel or
  ikan parang
375 ml (1$^1/_2$ cups) water
3 teaspoons sugar
1$^1/_2$ teaspoons salt
125 ml ($^1/_2$ cup) coconut
  cream
6 kaffir lime leaves, crushed

Spice Paste
300 g (10 oz) shallots
10 candlenuts
4 stalks lemongrass, inner
  bottom part only, sliced
4 thin slices galangal
6 red chillies, deseeded
125 ml ($^1/_2$ cup) water
  or fish stock

1 Poach the fish in the water for 12 to 15 minutes (it is cooked when the eyes turn opaque). Drain, reserving 125 ml ($^1/_2$ cup) of the fish liquid. When cool, flake the fish with a fork and discard the bones.
2 Grind all the Spice Paste ingredients until fine. Combine with the fish, sugar, salt, coconut cream and the fish liquid. Over a low heat, gently stir-fry the mixture in a wok, stirring constantly. When the fish is dry and crisp, add the lime leaves, stirring until the leaves shrivel. Remove from the heat. Cool and store in a bottle. Use as a filling for sandwiches or serve with rice or rice porridge.

Serves 4
Preparation time: 20 mins
Cooking time: 15 mins

Dried Prawn Sambal

200 g (7 oz) dried
  prawns, soaked in
  warm water to soften
2 tablespoons oil
1 teaspoon sugar
2 tablespoons lime juice

Spice Paste
4 candlenuts
8 dried red chillies,
  deseeded
1 teaspoon dried shrimp
  paste (*belachan*)
2 shallots
2 tablespoons water

Serves 4
Preparation time: **10 mins**
Cooking time: **30 mins**

1 Drain the dried prawns, strain and remove any hard bits. Blend or pound until smooth.
2 Blend all the Spice Paste ingredients until smooth. Heat the oil in a wok and stir-fry the Spice Paste until fragrant, then add the sugar and lime juice. Cook for 2 minutes.
3 Add the dried prawns and mix well. Reduce the heat and cook, stirring constantly, for about 8 minutes until the prawns are dry, brown and fragrant.
4 Cool and transfer them into glass jars or bottles. Store in the refrigerator. Serve with plain rice, rice porridge or as filling for sandwiches.

Dried prawns are tiny, orange prawns that have been dried in the sun. They come in different sizes. Available in Asian markets, they should look orangy-pink and plump; avoid any with a grayish appearance or an unpleasant smell. Dried prawns will keep for several months.

Indian Fish and Potato Patties

300 g (10 oz) fish steaks such as *ikan parang* (wolf herring), *ikan kurau* (threadfin), or mackerel (*ikan kembong*)
2 medium potatoes (200g/7 oz), peeled and boiled until soft
1 teaspoon salt
Pinch of ground white pepper
1 tablespoon chopped, deseeded green finger-length chillies
1 teaspoon chopped ginger
125 ml (¹/₂ cup) oil
1 egg, beaten

1 Clean the fish, then steam until cooked. The fish will flake easily with a fork when done.
2 Mash the boiled potatoes.
3 Remove the bones from the fish, then mix with the mashed potato, salt, pepper, green chillies and ginger.
4 Divide the mixture into 8 balls, then flatten slightly to form cakes.
5 Heat the oil in a flat frying-pan. Dip the patties in the beaten egg and fry gently until brown.
6 Serve as a snack or with plain rice.

Makes 8 small cakes
Preparation time: 20 mins
Cooking time: 30 mins

Black Soy Fish Steaks

1 kg (2 lbs) fish steaks such as *ikan kurau* (threadfin) or mackerel (*ikan kembong*)
1 teaspoon salt
4 tablespoons oil
1 medium onion, sliced
2 red finger-length chillies, deseeded and sliced
2 tablespoons black soy sauce
125 ml ($^1/_2$ cup) water
$^1/_4$ teaspoon ground white pepper
$^1/_2$ teaspoon sugar

1 Rub the salt into the fish and set aside for 15 minutes.
2 Heat 2 tablespoons of the oil in a wok until hot, then fry the fish on both sides until brown. Drain and set aside.
3 Heat the remaining oil and gently stir-fry the onions and chillies until the onions are soft.
5 Quickly stir in the black soy sauce into the pan to lightly caramelise it before adding the water, pepper and sugar.
6 Bring to a boil, then add the fish. Simmer for 3 minutes or until the fish is done.
7 Serve hot with plain rice or porridge.

Serves 4
Preparation time: **15 mins**
Cooking time: **10 mins**

Otak-Otak (Fish Cakes Roasted in Banana Leaves)

500 g (1 lb) fish steaks such as *ikan tenggiri* (Spanish mackerel), deboned and pounded or blended
250 ml (1 cup) coconut cream
250 ml (1 cup) water
2 teaspoons finely chopped kaffir lime leaves
1 1/2 teaspoons salt

Banana leaves or coconut leaves, for wrapping

Spice Paste
10 shallots
2 stalks lemongrass, tender inner part of bottom third only, sliced
6 cm (2 1/2 in) galangal
6 cm (2 1/2 in) old turmeric root

2 tablespoons fried grated fresh coconut
12 red finger-length chillies, deseeded
4 candlenuts
1 tablespoon dried shrimp paste (*belachan*)
250 ml (1 cup) water

Serves 4
Preparation time: **2 hours**
Cooking time: **30 mins**

1 Prepare the Spice Paste by blending all the ingredients until fine.
2 Mix the fish paste with the Spice Paste, coconut cream and lime leaves.
3 Blanch the banana leaves to soften them, then cut into 30-cm (12-in) squares.
4 Spoon 3 heaped tablespoons of the fish paste onto a leaf, and fold into a flat parcel about 3 x 6 cm (1 1/4 x 2 1/2 in) in size.
5 Secure the ends with bamboo toothpicks.
6 Cook for about 5 minutes on a hotplate or under a grill.
7 Serve as a snack, with *nasi lemak* or plain rice, or as a sandwich filling.

Banana leaves and coconut leaves are often used in Asian cuisine to wrap food or to line trays before cooking, much as waxed paper or aluminium foil are. This imparts a subtle fragrance to the food.

Variations on *Otak-Otak* include mixing some of the fish paste with shelled prawns, small cubes of fish, small pieces of meaty fish head, or thin slices of fish cake.

Prepare the Spice Paste and the pounded fish.

Fold the leaves into flat parcels and secure the ends with toothpicks.

Clear Fish Head Soup

2 tablespoons oil
6 cm (2$^1/_2$ in) old ginger, peeled and smashed
2 teaspoons chopped garlic
2 red finger-length chillies, deseeded and sliced
10 stalks Chinese celery, rinsed clean and left whole
1 teaspoon salt
Pinch of ground white pepper
1 medium *ikan kurau* (threadfin) fish head (1$^1/_2$ kgs/
   3 lbs) halved
1$^1/_4$ litres (5 cups) water
20 g ($^1/_2$ cup) chopped coriander leaves
20 g ($^1/_2$ cup) chopped Chinese celery
20 g ($^1/_2$ cup) chopped spring onions

1 Heat the oil in a large saucepan or claypot and gently stir-fry the smashed ginger, chopped garlic and chillies for 2 minutes.
2 Add the Chinese celery, salt, pepper, the fish head and sufficient water to cover it.
3 Bring to a boil, reduce the heat and simmer for 10 minutes.
4 Garnish with the chopped coriander leaves, Chinese celery and spring onions. Serve piping hot as a soup with pieces of fish head in the bowl.

Serves 4
Preparation time: **15 mins**
Cooking time: **15 mins**

Classic Singapore Fish Head Curry

3 tablespoons oil
75 g ($^1/_4$ cup) tamarind pulp soaked in 60 ml ($^1/_4$ cup) water, mashed and strained for juice
1 teaspoon salt
1 medium fish head, (1$^1/_2$ kgs/3 lbs), such as *ikan kurau* (threadfin) or *ikan merah* (red snapper), split in half
1 large tomato, quartered
500 g (1 lb) ladies fingers (okra), trimmed
500 ml (2 cups) water
2 tablespoons coconut cream + 125 ml ($^1/_2$ cup) water

Spice Paste #1
10 shallots
1 clove garlic, sliced
6 cm (2$^1/_2$ in) old ginger
2 tablespoons water

Spice Paste #2
3 tablespoons coriander powder
1 teaspoon cumin powder
1 tablespoon fennel powder
$^1/_2$ teaspoon turmeric powder
2 tablespoons chilli powder
2 tablespoons water

1 Blend all the Spice Paste #1 ingredients and set aside in a bowl, then mix together all the Spice Paste #2 ingredients and set aside in a separate bowl.
2 Heat the oil in a large saucepan and stir-fry Spice Paste #1 until fragrant. Then add Spice Paste #2 to the pan and stir-fry the combined Spice Pastes until fragrant.
3 Stir in the tamarind juice, salt and fish head into the stir-fried Spice Pastes. Cover and bring to a boil.
4 Add the tomato and ladies fingers and simmer for 5 minutes, or until the ladies fingers are done.
5 Add the coconut milk and remove from the heat just as the curry reaches a boil. Leave to stand for a few hours to allow the flavours to develop. Serve with plain rice.

Serves 4
Preparation time: **30 mins**
Cooking time: **20 mins**

Teochew Steamed Fish

2 medium whole pom-frets (*ikan bawal putih*) (1 kg/2 lbs)
1 tablespoon fermented bean paste (*tau cheo*)
1 tablespoon rice wine (see note)
1 tablespoon soy sauce
60 ml (¹/₄ cup) chicken stock
2 teaspoons sesame oil
1 red finger-length chilli, deseeded and sliced
4 dried black Chinese mushrooms (see note)
10 thin slices old ginger, sliced into thin strips
6 spring onions, cut into lengths
35 g (³/₄ cup) coriander leaves

Serves 4
Preparation time: 15 mins
Cooking time: 10 mins

1 Gut the fish, then trim away the fins with scissors and scrape off any remaining scales.
2 Rinse the fermented bean paste, then mash with a fork or pound until fine.
3 Mix the rice wine, soy sauce, stock and sesame oil together.
4 Place the fish in a flat heat-proof dish and pour over the mixed ingredients, coating the fish well to season it. Spread the fermented bean paste evenly under and over the fish.
5 Place the sliced chilli, mushrooms, ginger and half the spring onions and coriander leaves on top.
6 Steam the fish in a covered wok for about 10 minutes. The fish is done when the eyes turn opaque and a toothpick stuck into the thickest part enters easily.
7 Garnish with the remaining coriander leaves and spring onions and serve immediately.

Dried black Chinese mushrooms are used widely in Chinese cooking. They must be soaked in hot water to soften before use. The stems are removed and discarded; only the caps are used. Shiitake mushrooms are a good substitute. They are easily available from the dry food sections in wet markets and supermarkets.

Rice wine is used frequently in Chinese cooking. Japanese sake, mirin or a dry sherry may all be used as substitutes.

Trim and descale the pomfret.

Cover the fish well with the mixed ingredients before steaming.

Sweet and Sour Whole Fish

1 whole grouper (*ikan kerapu*, (1 kg/2 lbs)), cleaned and scaled
$1/2$ teaspoon salt
40 g ($1/3$ cup) rice flour (see note)
500 ml (2 cups) oil

Sauce
125 ml ($1/2$ cup) tomato sauce (ketchup)
$1 1/2$ tablespoons rice vinegar (see note)
1 tablespoon sugar
1 tablespoon garlic chilli sauce (bottled)
$1/4$ teaspoon salt
1 teaspoon cornstarch
125 ml ($1/2$ cup) water
2 tablespoons oil
1 small onion, cut into small wedges
$1/2$ green bell pepper, cut into rings or wedges
1 red finger-length chilli, deseeded and sliced
4 slices canned pineapple, cut into wedges
1 sprig coriander leaves
5 spring onions, cut into lengths

Serves 4
Preparation time: **20 mins**
Cooking time: **15 mins**

1 Rub the salt into the fish, then coat it with the rice flour.
2 Heat the oil in a wok and fry the fish until crisp. Place the fish on a serving dish.
3 To prepare the Sauce, first combine the tomato sauce, rice vinegar, sugar, garlic chilli sauce, salt, cornstarch and water in a bowl, then mix well and set aside.
4 Heat 2 tablespoons of oil in a saucepan and stir-fry the onion and bell pepper for 2 minutes. Add the chilli and pineapple and cook for a further 1 minute.
5 Add the reserved liquid mixture to the saucepan. bring to a boil, then reduce the heat and simmer until the Sauce thickens. Pour the hot Sauce over the fish, garnish with the spring onions and coriander leaves and serve at once.

Rice flour is made from ground uncooked rice grains. It is used to make the dough or batter for many desserts. Fresh rice flour was traditionally made by soaking rice grains overnight and then slowly grinding it in a stone mill. The same result may be achieved by grinding soaked rice grains in a blender. Rice flour is sold in powdered form in packets in supermarkets and Asian specialty shops.

Rice vinegar is mild and fragrant, and is the preferred vinegar throughout Asia. Chinese brands are inexpensive and widely available, while the Japanese rice vinegar, used in sushi, is sweeter and milder.

Ready-made bottled **garlic chilli sauce** is widely available from supermarkets and Asian foodstores.

Grilled Whole Fish with Sambal Belachan

1 kg (2 lbs) whole *ikan terubok* (Chinese herring)
$^{1}/_{2}$ teaspoon salt
1 large banana leaf (page 27)

Dipping Sauce
1 tablespoon Sambal Belachan (page 24)
5 shallots, thinly sliced
2 teaspoons sugar

1 $^{1}/_{2}$ tablespoons lime juice
2 tablespoons black soy sauce

1 Leave the scales on the fish but remove the innards and rub the inside with salt. Rinse.
2 Wrap the fish in a double layer of banana leaves and grill or bake in a hot oven for 20 minutes or until done, turning once after 10 minutes.
3 To serve, remove the banana leaf and peel the skin and scales from the fish, starting from the tail. It will come off in one large piece.
4 Mix all the Dipping Sauce ingredients together in a small side dish. Serve the grilled fish with the Dipping Sauce and steamed rice.

Serves 4
Preparation time: **10 mins**
Cooking time: **20 mins**

Fish Tikka (Baked Fish Marinated in Yoghurt and Spices)

500 g (1 lb) fish steaks such as *ikan kurau* (threadfin), *ikan teng-giri* (Spanish mackerel), or *ikan merah* (red snapper), deboned and cubed
2 tablespoons oil

Marinade
125 ml ($^1/_2$ cup) plain yoghurt
1 small garlic, finely pounded
1 teaspoon salt
Pinch of ground white pepper

2 teaspoons chilli powder
6 cm ($2^1/_2$ in) old ginger, pounded and squeezed to yield $^1/_2$ tablespoon ginger juice
1 lemon, quartered

1 Combine all the Marinade ingredients, then stir in the cubes of fish. Refrigerate overnight.
2 Lay the cubes of fish flat in a baking dish. Sprinkle with 2 tablespoons of oil, then place under a hot grill for 4 minutes, turning the fish after 2 minutes.
3 Serve hot with a wedge of lemon.

Serves 4
Preparation time: 15 mins   Cooking time: 30 mins

Fish with Pineapple

500 g (1 lb) sliced fish such as pony fish (*ikan kekek*), or *ikan parang* (wolf herring)
1 small fresh pineapple (400 g/14 oz)
1 tablespoon tamarind pulp soaked in 125 ml ($^1/_2$ cup) water, mashed and strained for juice

2 tablespoons oil
1 teaspoon salt
1 litre (4 cups) water

Spice Paste
10 shallots
6 red finger-length chillies, deseeded
6 cm ($2^1/_2$ in) fresh old turmeric
$^1/_2$ tablespoon dried shrimp paste (*belachan*)
2 stalks lemongrass, tender inner part of bottom third only
125 ml ($^1/_2$ cup) water

Serves 4
Preparation time: **30 mins**
Cooking time: **10 mins**

1 Peel and quarter the pineapple, removing the hard centre core. Cut into wedges.
2 Blend all the Spice Paste ingredients until fine. Heat the oil in a saucepan and stir-fry the Spice Paste for about 3 minutes until fragrant. Add the tamarind juice, pineapple slices, salt and water and bring to a boil. Lower the heat and simmer until the pineapple slices turn translucent.
3 Add the fish and simmer for 10 minutes or until the fish is done.

Tips for Frying Fish

The art of frying fish neatly is to have the oil hot enough and to know when to turn the fish. Turn it too soon and the skin gets stuck on the pan, leaving you an unattractive mottled fish. Turn too late and the fish is overcooked or even burnt.

• The oil should be very hot before the fish is added.

• To check if the oil is hot enough, press the tip of a wooden chopstick to the bottom of the wok. It should sizzle vigorously.

• To keep the temperature constant, do not add too many pieces at once.

• When the edges of the fish change colour, it is time to turn. Alternatively, nudge the fish with your spatula. If the fish shifts easily, it is ready for turning.

• To cope with spattering oil, have a wok cover handy. Just pop the cover over the pan. There is also a special sieve-like cover with a handle that is perfect for preventing oil spatters from frying fish. If you cover the wok, note that the fish will cook faster.

• To minimize spattering oil, pat the fish dry with paper towels before it is put into the hot oil.

Fried Fish Steaks with Chilli

1 teaspoon salt
1 tablespoon chilli
  powder
500 g (1 lb) fish steaks,
  such as *ikan kurau*
  (threadfin), *ikan merah*
  (red snapper) or *ikan
  tenggiri* (Spanish
  mackerel)
3 tablespoons oil

1 Combine the salt and chilli powder, then rub the mixture into the fish. Set aside for at least 30 minutes.
2 Heat the oil in a frying-pan until hot, pat the fish dry, then fry a couple of pieces at a time until done.
3 Serve with plain rice.

Serves 4
Preparation time: 30 mins
Cooking time: 10 mins

Fried Whole Fish with Turmeric and Salt

1 kg (2 lbs) whole yel-
  low fish (*ikan kuning*)
1 teaspoon salt
$1/2$ tablespoon turmeric
  powder
3 tablespoons oil

Sambal Belachan
3 red finger-length chillies, deseeded
1 tablespoon dried
  shrimp paste
  (*belachan*), roasted
1 teaspoon sugar
$1/4$ teaspoon salt
1 tablespoon lime juice

1 To prepare the Sambal Belachan, grind the chillies and dried shrimp paste in a mortar. Then add the sugar, salt and lime juice, and mix well.
2 If the fish is small (finger length), clean it by cutting off the head and belly. If using a larger fish, leave it whole and clean and gut in the normal way.
3 Combine the salt and turmeric powder and rub into the fish. Set aside for at least 30 minutes, or refrigerate overnight.
4 Heat the oil in a wok. Pat the fish dry with a paper towel, then fry the fish in small batches until golden brown (see tips on page 23).
5 Serve with plain rice and Sambal Belachan or with *nasi lemak*.

Serves 4
Preparation time: 20 mins
Cooking time: 20 mins

Fried Fish with Candlenuts and Turmeric

500 g (1 lb) whole
  mackerel (*ikan kem-
  bong*)
2 candlenuts
6 cm (2 1/2 in) fresh
  turmeric
1 teaspoon salt
3 tablespoons oil

1 Scale the fish and remove the innards and gills.
2 Pound the candlenuts together with the turmeric to
a fine pulp. Mix with the salt, then rub the mixture
onto the fish. Set aside for at least 30 minutes.
3 Heat the oil in a wok until hot, then fry the fish, a
few at a time, until brown. Take care when turning the
fish to avoid the candlenut crust falling off.

Serves 4
Preparation time: 20 mins
Cooking time: 15 mins

Asam Fried Fish Steaks

500 g (1 lb) fish steaks
  such as *ikan tenggiri*
  (Spanish mackerel),
  mackerel (*ikan kem-
  bong*)
2 tablespoons tamarind
  pulp soaked in 1 table-
  spoon water
1 teaspoon salt
2 tablespoons oil

1 If using whole fish, remove the innards and rinse
the fish. Pat the fish dry with paper towels.
2 Mix the soaking tamarind pulp with salt and rub
into the fish. Allow to stand for at least 30 minutes, or
keep refrigerated overnight.
3 Rinse the tamarind off the fish and pat dry with a
paper towel.
4 Heat the oil in a frying-pan until smoking and fry
the fish until golden brown on both sides.

Serves 4
Preparation time: 30 mins
Cooking time: 10 mins

Barbequed Sambal Stingray

1 tablespoon tamarind pulp soaked in 3 table- spoons water, mashed and strained for juice
3 tablespoons oil
1 teaspoon salt
2 tablespoons coconut cream
1 kg (2 lbs) stingray (*ikan pari*), cut into 4 portions
Fresh banana leaves or aluminium foil (see note)
Half a lemon or some small limes

Spice Paste
10 shallots
2 cloves garlic
$1/_2$ tablespoon dried shrimp paste (*belachan*)
2 tablespoons chilli powder
2 slices galangal
2 tablespoons water

1 Grind all the Spice Paste ingredients until fine. Heat the oil in a saucepan and stir-fry the Spice Paste until fragrant, then add the salt and tamarind juice and cook for a further 2 minutes.

2 Add the coconut cream and cook over low heat for about 1 minute until the mixture thickens. Remove from the heat and set aside to cool.

3 Coat the stingray pieces with the spice mixture and place each piece on a large banana leaf or piece of kitchen foil. Spread any remaining spice mixture over the string ray.

4 Roll up the leaf or foil, then grill or barbecue the parcels for 8 to 10 minutes. The length of time required will depend on the thickness of the stingray.

5 Serve hot with a wedge of lemon.

Banana leaves are often used in Asian cuisine to wrap food or to line trays before cooking, much as waxed paper or aluminium foil are. This imparts a subtle fragrance to the food.

Serves 4
Preparation time: 20 mins
Cooking time: 20 mins

Prawn Dumpling Soup

20 circular prawn dumpling (*shui jiao*) wrappers
A small bowl of water for sealing wrappers

Filling
16–20 fresh medium prawns (about 400 g/14 oz), peeled and roughly chopped
$1/_2$ teaspoon salt
1 teaspoon cornstarch
2 tablespoons chopped water chestnuts
1 tablespoon chopped spring onions
Ground white pepper to taste
1 teaspoon sesame oil

Soup
2 tablespoons oil
2 cloves garlic, chopped
$1^1/_4$ litres (5 cups) prawn, fish or chicken stock
100 g (4 oz) mustard greens, cut into lengths
1 tablespoon chopped spring onions
1 tablespoon chopped coriander leaves
1 teaspoon sesame oil

1 Combine all the Filling ingredients and mix well.
2 Place 2 heaped teaspoons of the Filling onto a circular wrapper. Moisten half of the circular edge with a dab of water and fold the wrapper over into a semicircle.
3 To prepare the Soup, heat 2 tablespoons of oil in a saucepan and stir-fry the garlic until fragrant. Add the stock, salt and mustard greens and bring to a boil.
4 When the Soup comes to a boil, add the wontons and boil for 5 minutes then stir in 1 teaspoon sesame oil and remove the Soup from the heat.
5 Garnish with the chopped spring onions and coriander leaves and serve at once.

Serves 4
Preparation time: 30 mins
Cooking time: 10 mins

Mustard Greens, also known as *chye sim*, *choy sum* or Chinese Flowering Cabbage, is a leafy green vegetable with crisp crunchy stems. Available in supermarkets in Asia, chye sim is now increasingly available in Western countries too. Substitute any other leafy greens.

Dumpling wrappers, also known as wonton wrappers are square or round wrappers made of flour, eggs and water. The thin ones are used for soups while the thicker ones are used for frying. Sold in the refrigerated or freezer sections of supermarkets.

Combine the spring onions, prawns and water chestnuts for the Filling.

Fill the round wrapper then fold in half to form a semicircle.

Prawn Patties

650 g (1¹/₂ lbs) fresh
  prawns, shelled
3 water chestnuts,
  peeled and finely
  chopped
2 teaspoons cornstarch
1 tablespoon egg white
Pinch of ground white
  pepper
¹/₂ teaspoon salt
1 tablespoon chopped
  spring onions
60 g (1 cup) fine
  breadcrumbs
500 ml (2 cups) oil
1 small cucumber, sliced
2 large tomatoes, cut
  into small wedges

1 Chop or blend the prawns until smooth. Combine with the water chestnuts, cornstarch, egg white, pepper, salt and spring onions.
2 Divide the mixture into 8 balls, then flatten them into patties. You may need to moisten your hands with a little water to prevent the patties sticking. Coat the patties with the breadcrumbs.
3 Heat the oil in a frying-pan and deep-fry the patties until golden brown.
4 Garnish with the cucumber and tomatoes. Serve with plain rice, or as a snack/appetiser with chilli sauce on the side.

Serves 4
Preparation time: 20 mins
Cooking time: 10 mins

Prawn Toast

8 slices bread of your choice
500 g (1 lb) fresh prawns, shelled
1 teaspoon cornstarch
1/2 teaspoon salt
2 tablespoons chopped spring onions
Ground white pepper to taste
250 ml (1 cup) oil
30 g (2/3 cup) white sesame seeds

1 Finely chop the prawns. Combine with the cornstarch, salt, pepper and spring onions and toss well.
2 Cut each slice of bread into 3 fingers. Divide the prawn mixture and spread it on the bread fingers.
3 Spread the sesame seeds on a plate and press the bread, prawn side down, onto the seeds to coat it.
4 Heat the oil in a wok and, when hot, fry the bread, prawn side down, until the prawns are cooked. Turn and brown the other side of the bread.
5 Serve with chilli or tomato sauce.

Serves 4
Preparation time: **10 mins**
Cooking time: **10 mins**

Prawn Spring Rolls

20 square plain spring roll wrappers (each 20cm/ 8-in), quartered
500 ml (2 cups) oil
Leftover beaten egg

Filling
2 tablespoons oil
500 g (1 lb) fresh prawns, shelled and chopped
3 water chestnuts, peeled and chopped finely
1 teaspoon soy sauce
Ground white pepper to taste
$1/2$ teaspoon salt
1 tablespoon beaten egg
2 tablespoons chopped spring onions
1 tablespoon Crispy Fried Shallots (page 56)
1 tablespoon Crispy Fried Garlic (page 56)

Serves 4
Preparation time: **45 mins**
Cooking time: **10 mins**

1 To prepare the Filling, heat the oil in a saucepan and stir-fry the chopped prawns until they change colour. Add the water chestnuts and season with the soy sauce, pepper and salt. If the prawns are watery, transfer the Filling to a bowl and boil off the liquid (the Filling should be dry but not overcooked). Then add 1 tablespoon beaten egg, spring onions, Crispy Fried Shallots and Crispy Fried Garlic, stirring quickly to mix well.
2 Roll 1 heaped teaspoonful of the Filling in a spring roll wrapper, sealing the loose end to the roll with a dab of leftover beaten egg.
3 Heat the oil until hot, then deep-fry the rolls until the wrapper is brown and crisp, about 2 minutes (do not to overheat the oil).

Roll the Filling in the wrapper, fold in the sides and continue to roll, seal with egg.

Garlic Pepper Prawns

1 kg (2 lbs) fresh
  medium prawns
8 cloves garlic, finely
  pounded
2 teaspoons ground
  white pepper
1 teaspoon salt
3 tablespoons oil

Serves 4
Preparation time: 30 mins
Cooking time: 5 mins

1 Trim the prawn whiskers and devein the prawns by making a slit along the centre of the back (leaving the shell intact). Remove the black intestinal tract and rinse the prawns.
2 Mix the garlic, pepper and salt together, then season the prawns with the mixture, taking care to place some of the mixture inside the slits. Set aside for 30 minutes or more.
3 Heat the oil in a wok and quickly stir-fry the prawns until they turn pink.
4 Serve with plain rice.

Tamarind Prawns (Asam Prawns)

1 kg (2 lbs) fresh
medium prawns
75 g ($^1/_4$ cup) tamarind
pulp
60 ml ($^1/_4$ cup) water
1 teaspoon salt
4 tablespoons oil

Serves 4
Preparation time: **2 hours**
Cooking time: **10 mins**

1 Trim the prawn whiskers. Remove the shells but leave the heads and tails intact. Make a slit along the centre of the back and remove the black intestinal tract.

2 Mix the tamarind pulp with the water and salt, stir and strain, then discard the seeds. Stir the prawns into the tamarind water and set aside for at least 2 hours, or overnight in the refrigerator.

3 Just before frying, rinse the prawns quickly in cold water, then squeeze them dry. If necessary, pat dry with paper towels.

4 Heat the oil in a wok then fry the prawns, stirring constantly, until brown.

Prawns with Cashew Nuts

500 g (1 lb) fresh
  prawns, shelled
3 tablespoons oil
100 g ($^1/_2$ cup) cashew
  nuts
4 slices ginger
1 teaspoon chopped
  garlic
1 medium carrot, cut
  into fine strips
6 stalks celery, sliced
$^1/_2$ green bell pepper,
  cut into chunks
1 red finger-length chilli,
  sliced
4 spring onions, cut into
  lengths
1 sprig coriander leaves

Seasoning
1 egg white
Pinch of ground white
  pepper
1 teaspoon rice wine
$^1/_2$ teaspoon cornstarch
1 teaspoon soy sauce
1 teaspoon sesame oil

Sauce
125 ml ($^1/_2$ cup) chicken
  stock
2 teaspoons sesame oil
2 teaspoons rice wine
  (page 16)
$^1/_2$ tablespoon soy sauce
2 teaspoons cornstarch
1 teaspoon sugar
Ground white pepper

1 Combine all the Seasoning ingredients and mix
well. Coat the prawns and marinate for 30 minutes.
2 Prepare the Sauce by mixing all the ingredients well,
then set aside.
3 Heat the oil in a wok and stir-fry the cashew nuts
until lightly browned. Remove and set aside.
4 Stir-fry the ginger and garlic until fragrant. Add the
carrot, celery, bell pepper and chilli and cook for a
further 5 minutes.
5 Add the seasoned prawns and cook for about
2 minutes or until the prawns turn pink.
6 Pour in the Sauce mixture and stir over high heat
until it comes to a boil, then remove from the heat.
7 Toss in the cashew nuts and spring onions and
garnish with the coriander leaves. Serve hot.

Serves 4
Preparation time: 20 mins
Cooking time: 10 mins

Prawns in Black Bean Sauce

2 tablespoons oil
2 tablespoons salted
black beans, rinsed
and mashed (see note)
1 tablespoon chopped
fresh red chillies
3 cloves garlic, chopped
2 slices old ginger
500 g (1 lb) fresh
prawns, peeled with
tails intact
5 stalks spring onions,
chopped

Sauce
60 ml (¹/₄ cup) tomato
sauce (ketchup)
125 ml (¹/₂ cup) water
or chicken stock
1 teaspoon soy sauce
1 teaspoon sesame oil
¹/₄ teaspoon salt
2 teaspoons cornstarch
¹/₂ teaspoon sugar
Ground white pepper to
taste

1 Prepare the Sauce by mixing all the ingredients well, then set aside.

2 Heat the oil in a saucepan and stir-fry the black beans, chillies, garlic and ginger until fragrant and translucent.

3 Add the prawns and cook for 2 minutes or until they turn pink. Then add the Sauce mixture, bring everything to a boil, then remove from the heat.

4 Garnish with the chopped spring onions.

5 Serve hot with plain rice.

Salted black beans are also called fermented black beans or Chinese black beans. They are soybeans that have been fermented and preserved in salt, hence their strong, salty flavour. Mainly used to season a number of dishes, especially fish, beef and chicken, they are sold in packets or cans and can be kept for several months if stored in the refrigerator. Soak in warm water for 30 minutes before using, to remove excess salt.

Serves 4
Preparation time: **15 mins**
Cooking time: **10 mins**

Peel the prawns, keeping the tails intact.

Salted black beans should be mashed first.

Dry Masala Prawns

1 kg (2 lbs) fresh large prawns
1 tablespoon tamarind pulp soaked in 2 tablespoons
  water, mashed and strained for juice
4 tablespoons oil
200 g (1$^1/_3$ cups) coarsely sliced onions
2 sprigs curry leaves (*daun kari*)
$^1/_2$ teaspoon salt
125 ml ($^1/_2$ cup) coconut cream
60 ml ($^1/_4$ cup) water

Spice Paste
1$^1/_2$ tablespoons cumin powder
1 tablespoon chilli powder
60 ml ($^1/_4$ cup) water

1 Trim the prawn whiskers and devein the prawns by
making a slit along the centre of the back and removing
the black intestinal tract (leave the shell intact). Rinse
the prawns.
2 Mix together the Spice Paste ingredients, then heat
the oil in a saucepan and fry the Spice Paste, onions
and curry leaves for 5 minutes or until fragrant.
3 Add the salt, tamarind juice and prawns and mix
well together. Simmer until the prawns turn pink.
Add the coconut cream, mixed with the water, and
remove from the heat just as it reaches a boil.
4 Serve with plain rice.

> **Curry leaves** comprise sprigs of 8–15, dark green
> leaves and are used to flavor Indian curries. Fresh curry
> leaves should be used within a few days of purchase.
> Dried curry leaves keep well if stored in a dry place.
> There is no good substitute.Curry leaves are available
> in wet markets.

Serves 4
Preparation time: **10 mins**
Cooking time: **10 mins**

Baked Prawns with Glass Noodles

4 stalks coriander leaves with roots
6 cm (2¹/₂ in) old ginger, peeled and smashed
2 tablespoons oil
3 cloves garlic, chopped
1 teaspoon coriander powder
1 teaspoon ground white pepper
250 ml (1 cup) chicken stock
1 tablespoon fish sauce
¹/₂ teaspoon black soy sauce
100 g (4 oz) dried glass noodles (*tang hoon*), soaked in water for 15 minutes to soften, drained (see note)
1 kg (2 lbs) fresh large prawns

Serves 4
Preparation time: **20 mins**
Cooking time: **15 mins**

1 Preheat the oven to 180°C (350°F).

2 Cut the roots off the coriander stalks about 4 cm (1¹/₂ in) from the bottom. Clean the roots, then smash them with the back of a cleaver. Chop the coriander leaves and set aside for garnishing.

3 Heat the oil in a large casserole dish and stir-fry the garlic, coriander roots, ginger, coriander powder and pepper for 5 minutes until fragrant.

4 Add the chicken stock, fish sauce, black soy sauce and glass noodles. Bring to a boil, then turn off the heat.

5 Add the prawns, cover the casserole and bake for about 10 minutes until the prawns are pink (the exact time depends on the size of the prawns).

6 Garnish with the chopped coriander leaves and serve hot with plain rice.

Glass noodles, also known as *tang hoon*, are thin, clear strands made from mung bean starch and water. Soak in hot water for 15 minutes to soften. Available from Asian food stores.

Fish sauce, is made from salted, fermented fish or prawns. Good quality fish sauce is golden-brown in colour and has a salty tang. It is used in the same way as the Chinese use soy sauce.

Look for coriander with roots still intact.

Add the prawns to the casserole last.

Stuffed Squid with Clear Soup

500 g (1 lb) fresh small
squid (*sotong*)
1 tablespoon oil
2 cloves garlic, chopped
1¼ litres (5 cups) pork
or chicken stock
50 g (2 oz) dried glass
noodles (*tang hoon*),
soaked in water for
15 minutes to soften,
drained (see note)
1 teaspoon salt
Pinch of ground white
pepper
2 stalks Chinese celery,
chopped

Filling
50 g (¼ cup) minced
pork
50 g (⅕ cup) fresh
shelled prawns,
chopped
1 tablespoon dried salt
fish (*ikan kurau*), finely
chopped (see note)
Pinch of salt
1 teaspoon cornstarch
1 tablespoon chopped
spring onion
Ground white pepper to
taste

1 Clean the squid, keeping the bodies whole (see note below).
2 Combine all the Filling ingredients and mix well. Half-fill the squid with the Filling (this allows for shrinkage of the squid during cooking) and seal the squid with toothpicks.
3 Heat the oil in a saucepan and stir-fry the garlic until fragrant. Add the stock and bring to a boil.
4 Add the glass noodles and simmer for 5 minutes, until the noodles are done.
5 Add the stuffed squid and the tentacles. Simmer for 6 minutes or until the Filling is cooked.
7 Add the chopped Chinese celery.
8 Serve hot with plain rice or as a soup.

Dried salt fish is used as a seasoning or condiment in Asian cuisine. It should be soaked in water before use to remove some of the salt. Slice and fry the fish until crisp.

Glass noodles, also known as *tang hoon*, are thin, clear strands made from mung bean starch and water. Soak in hot water for 15 minutes to soften. Available from Asian food stores.

To clean the squid, pull the heads off and discard the ink sacs, the stomachs and the plastic-like quills. Cut away the eyes, the knobbly beak and the round bead between the eyes. If the squid are being cut into rings or to be stuffed, insert a finger into the tube-like body and clean them out. If the squid are to be cut into squares, slit open and clean the inside. Rinse clean.

Serves 4
Preparation time: 20 mins
Cooking time: 15 mins

Sambal Squid

1 tablespoon tamarind pulp soaked in 2 tablespoons
  water, mashed and strained for juice
2 tablespoons oil
$^1/_2$ teaspoon salt
3 tablespoons coconut cream
500 g (1 lb) fresh squid, cleaned and cut into rings or
  squares (see note, page 45)
2 green finger-length chillies, deseeded and diced

Spice Paste
10 shallots
2 tablespoons chilli powder
1 teaspoon dried shrimp paste (*belachan*)
4 candlenuts
2 teaspoons fermented bean paste (*tau cheo*)
60 ml ($^1/_4$ cup) water

1 Blend all the Spice Paste ingredients until smooth,
then heat the oil in a saucepan and stir-fry the Spice
Paste until fragrant. Add the tamarind juice and salt
and cook until the oil rises to the surface. Add the
coconut cream and simmer until the oil appears again.
2 Add the squid and green chillies and stir well.
Simmer for about 2 minutes until the squid turns
opaque. Take care not to overcook the squid.
3 Serve hot with plain rice.

Serves 4
Preparation time: 20 mins
Cooking time: 5 mins

Squid with Oyster Sauce

500 g (1 lb) fresh squid
3 tablespoons oil
1 large onion, cut into wedges
3 cloves garlic, chopped
2 red finger-length chillies, deseeded and sliced
2 tablespoons oyster sauce (see note)
2 leeks (150 g/5 oz), sliced
$1/2$ teaspoon salt
$1/4$ teaspoon ground white pepper

Serves 4
Preparation time: **10 mins**
Cooking time: **10 mins**

1 Clean the squid (see note, page 45) and cut into rings or squares. If squares, score the inside with a sharp knife in a criss-cross pattern .
2 Heat the oil in a wok and stir-fry the onion, garlic and chillies for about 2 minutes until fragrant.
3 Add the oyster sauce and leek and stir-fry until the leek is soft and translucent.
4 Stir in the salt, pepper and squid and stir-fry for 2 minutes or until the squid turns opaque. Do not overcook the squid as it will become tough.
5 Serve hot with plain rice.

Oyster sauce is a sauce that is soy-based with oyster extract. Vegetarians should look for a version sold as "mushroom oyster sauce".

Scallops in Black Bean Sauce

500 g (1 lb) fresh
shucked scallops
1 small carrot, peeled
and cut into small sticks
1 teaspoon salted black
beans, rinsed and
mashed (page 38)
1 red finger-length chilli,
deseeded and
chopped

1 tablespoon chopped
garlic
4 slices ginger, chopped
2 tablespoons oil
$1/4$ teaspoon salt
1 spring onion, chopped

Sauce
125 ml ($1/2$ cup) water
or chicken stock

1 teaspoon soy sauce
2 teaspoons cornstarch
$1/4$ teaspoon sugar
Few drops sesame oil
Pinch of ground white
pepper

Serves 4
Preparation time: **15 mins**
Cooking time: **5 mins**

1 Prepare the Sauce by mixing all the ingredients well.
2 Heat the oil in a wok and stir-fry the black beans, garlic and chilli until fragrant.
3 Add the carrot and stir-fry for a couple of minutes. If the mixture starts to stick, sprinkle a bit of water into the pan.
4 Add the scallops and stir-fry until they turn opaque.
5 Stir the Sauce mixture well before adding it to the scallops. Stir, then add the chopped spring onions. Bring to a boil, then remove from the heat.

Clams in Garlic Sauce

1 kg (2 lbs) fresh clams
2 litres (8 cups) water
$1/4$ cup salt
2 tablespoons oil
2 teaspoons chopped
  ginger
3 cloves garlic, chopped
1 red finger-length chilli,
  deseeded and sliced
2 teaspoons soy sauce
$1/4$ teaspoon salt
1 tablespoon rice wine
  (page 16)

1 Soak the clams in 2 litres (8 cups) water with $1/4$ cup salt for several hours. Discard the water and rinse the clams well.
2 Heat the oil in a wok and stir-fry the ginger, garlic and chilli until fragrant.
3 Add the soy sauce and heat for 1 minute to caramelise the mixture.
4 Add the clams, $1/4$ teaspoon of salt and rice wine and stir-fry until the clams open.

Serves 4
Preparation time: **3 hours**
Cooking time: **10 mins**

Black Pepper Crab

2 tablespoons oil
250 ml (1 cup) water
1 1/2 teaspoon salt
2 kgs (4 lbs) fresh crabs,
cleaned and quartered

Spice Paste
6 cm (2 1/2 in) fresh
turmeric root
6 cm (2 1/2 in) old
ginger root
30 g (1/4 cup) black
peppercorns
1 small garlic

1 Pound all the Spice Paste ingredients together until fine, then heat the oil in a wok and stir-fry the Spice Paste until fragrant.

2 Add the water, salt and crab. Mix the crab and spices thoroughly. Cover and cook for 5 minutes or until the crabs change colour.

3 Serve hot.

Serves 4
Preparation time: **45 mins**
Cooking time: **15 mins**

Fragrant Steamed Mussels

1 kg (2 lbs) fresh mussels
500 ml (2 cups) fish
  stock
1 bunch coriander leaves
2 stalks lemongrass, ten-
  der inner part of bot-
  tom third only, bruised
2 slices galangal
2 bird's-eye chillies,
  halved
$^1/_4$ teaspoon salt

Sauce
1 tablespoon oil
1 tablespoon chopped
  garlic
1 teaspoon chopped
  ginger
1 tablespoon fish sauce
  (page 42)
2 teaspoons cornstarch
  mixed with 2 table-
  spoons water
2 tablespoons lime juice
1 sprig coriander leaves,
  chopped

1 Scrub the mussels under running cold water or in a large basin. Remove the beards from the base.

2 Heat the stock in a saucepan with the coriander leaves, lemongrass, galangal, chillies and salt until it comes to a boil.

3 Ladle $^1/_4$ cup of the stock into the base of a large skillet, or a wok, which has a lid, and arrange the mussels inside. Cover with the lid and cook over high heat for 2 to 3 minutes until the mussels opened their shells. Discard any which have remained tightly closed. You may need to do this in several batches if your wok is not large enough.

4 Drain the excess liquid from the mussel shells and wok into the stock, then strain and discard the lemongrass, chillies and coriander leaves.

5 If the mussels are large enough, discard the empty half-shells, then arrange the shell with the mussel flesh onto a serving platter.

6 To prepare the Sauce, heat the oil in a saucepan and stir-fry the garlic and ginger until fragrant. Pour in the stock and add the fish sauce and the cornstarch mixture. Stir until the sauce thickens. Finally mix in the lime juice. Pour the sauce over the mussels, garnish with chopped coriander leaves and serve hot.

Serves 4
Preparation time: **15 mins**   Cooking time: **10 mins**

Teochew Oyster Omelette

8 eggs
$^1/_2$ teaspoon salt
2 cloves garlic, chopped
1 tablespoon water
1 bunch spring onions,
  chopped
1 sprig coriander leaves,
  chopped
250 g (8 oz) fresh
  shelled oysters
1 tablespoon soy sauce
4 tablespoons oil

Chilli Sauce Dip
60 ml ($^1/_4$ cup) garlic
  chilli sauce (bottled)
2 tablespoons rice vinegar
  (page 58)
1 tablespoon chopped
  coriander leaves

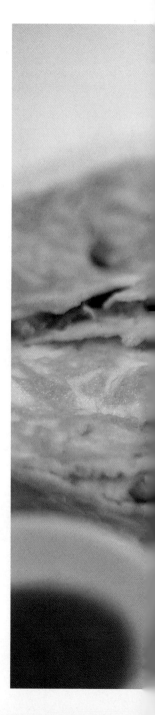

1 Prepare the Chilli Sauce Dip by mixing together all the ingredients in a small bowl and set aside.
2 Beat the eggs, salt, chopped garlic and water.
3 Set aside 2 tablespoons each of chopped spring onions and coriander for the garnish.
4 Heat 1 tablespoon of the oil in a frying-pan until hot. Pour in $^1/_4$ of the egg mixture and cook until the edges begin to brown.
5 Sprinkle the omelette with $^1/_4$ of the oysters, some soy sauce and some chopped spring onions and coriander leaves. Fold the omelette over and continue cooking for a futher 1 minute. Transfer to a serving plate.
6 Repeat steps 3 and 4 with remaining ingredients to make another three omelettes.
7 Garnish with the reserved coriander leaves. The omelette can also be served with plain rice.

The amount you can fry each time depends on the size of your frying-pan. If your pan is large enough, the eggs can be fried in three lots. The cooking time will also vary slightly.

Serves 4
Preparation time: **10 mins**
Cooking time: **10 mins**

Clear Crab and Meatball Soup

150 g (³/₄ cup) minced pork

200 g (1¹/₄ cups) shredded bamboo shoots (see note below)

60 g (¹/₂ cup) steamed crab meat (from 500 g/1 lb crabs)

2 teaspoons cornstarch

2 spring onions, finely chopped

¹/₄ teaspoon + ³/₄ teaspoon salt

¹/₄ teaspoon ground white pepper

1¹/₂ litres (6 cups) chicken stock

3 sprigs coriander leaves, chopped

1 tablespoon Crispy Fried Shallots

Serves 4
Preparation time: **40 mins**
Cooking time: **10 mins**

1 Combine the pork with 80 g (¹/₂ cup) of the bamboo shoots, crab meat, cornstarch, spring onions, ¹/₄ teaspoon salt and some pepper and mix well. Divide the mixture into 12 portions and roll into balls.
2 Bring the stock to a boil with the remaining ³/₄ teaspoon salt, bamboo shoots and white pepper.
3 Drop the crab meat-balls into the boiling soup and simmer for 5 minutes until they float to the surface.
4 Remove the soup from the heat and garnish with coriander leaves and Crispy Fried Shallots. Serve hot.

Use tinned bamboo shoots but boil for 30 minutes in several changes of water before shredding to get rid of the strong bamboo smell.

To obtain crabmeat, steam the crab until cooked, then remove the meat.

Crispy Fried Garlic or **Crispy Fried Shallots** are readily available in packets or jars in most supermarkets and Asian food stores. To make them at home, thinly slice several cloves of garlic or shallots as desired and stir-fry in hot oil over low heat for 1-2 minutes, stirring constantly, until golden brown and crispy.

Cut the bamboo shoots into thin shreds.

Classic Chilli Crab

2 tablespoons cornstarch
250 ml (1 cup) water
60 ml ($^1/_4$ cup) rice vinegar (see note)
1$^1/_2$ tablespoons sugar
1 teaspoon salt
250 ml (1 cup) water
4 tablespoons oil
2 kgs (4 lbs) fresh crabs, cleaned and quartered
1 egg, beaten

Spice Paste
6 red finger-length chillies, deseeded
6 cm (2$^1/_2$ in) old ginger
1 small garlic
2 tablespoons water

1 Mix the cornstarch with 250 ml (1 cup) water and set aside.
2 Combine the vinegar, sugar, and salt with the remaining water and set aside.
3 Blend all the Spice Paste ingredients until smooth then heat the oil in a wok and stir-fry the Spice Paste until fragrant.
4 Add the vinegar mixture and stir well.
5. Add the crabs then cover and cook for 5 minutes, or until they change colour.
6 Thicken the gravy with the cornstarch mixture and stir well. When the gravy comes to a boil, stir in the beaten egg.
7 Serve hot with some crusty French bread to soak up the gravy.

Rice vinegar is mild and fragrant, and is the preferred vinegar throughout Asia. Chinese brands are inexpensive and widely available, while the Japanese rice vinegar, used in sushi, is sweeter and milder.

For equally delicious **Chilli Lobster,** follow the same method and substitute lobster for the crab. The lobster should be chopped up to let the sauce soak in.

Serves 4
Preparation time: **45 mins**   Cooking time: **15 mins**

Indian Masala Crab

1 tablespoon tamarind pulp soaked in 125 ml ($^1/_2$ cup) water, mashed and strained for juice
2 tablespoons oil
1 large tomato, cubed
1 large onion, sliced
1 red finger-length chilli, deseeded and sliced
1 teaspoon salt
2 kgs (4 lbs) fresh crabs, cleaned and quartered
60 ml ($^1/_4$ cup) coconut cream mixed with
   60 ml ($^1/_4$ cup) water

Spice Paste
1 teaspoon cumin seeds
$^1/_2$ teaspoon cumin powder
1 teaspoon fennel powder
6 candlenuts, finely pounded
1 tablespoon chilli powder
2 teaspoons turmeric powder
2 tablespoons water

1 Combine all the Spice Paste ingredients and mix well, then heat the oil in a wok and stir-fry the Spice Paste until fragrant. Add the tomato and cook until soft.
2 Add the onion and sliced chilli and fry for 1 minute, then stir in the salt, crab and tamarind juice. Mix well, then cover and cook for 5 minutes or until the crabs change colour.
3 Add the coconut cream mixed with water, bring to a boil then remove from the heat.
5 Serve with rice or bread.

Serves 4
Preparation time: **45 mins**
Cooking time: **15 mins**

Slipper Lobster in Spicy Tomato Sauce

12 slipper lobsters
  (about 1 1/2 kgs /3 lbs)
6 cm (2 1/2 in) old
  ginger, sliced
1 medium onion, sliced
1 bunch spring onions,
  cut into lengths
2 tablespoons oil

Spicy Tomato Sauce
125 ml (1/2 cup) tomato
  sauce (ketchup)
60 ml (1/4 cup) garlic
  chilli sauce (bottled)
1 tablespoon cornstarch
250 ml (1 cup) water
1/2 teaspoon salt
1 tablespoon rice vinegar
  (see note)
2 teaspoons sesame oil

1 To prepare the lobsters, remove the heads by twisting them off from the body, leaving the main shells and tails intact. Then, using a pair of clean blunt-nosed pliers, twist off the plastic-like undershell or cut off with very sharp kitchen scissors.

2 Mix together all the Spicy Tomato Sauce ingredients and set aside.

3 Heat the oil in a wok and stir-fry the ginger slices and onion until translucent.

4 Add the lobsters and Spicy Tomato Sauce and cook for about 5 minutes or until the lobsters change colour.

5 Add the spring onions and heat through.

6 Serve with plain rice.

Rice vinegar is mild and fragrant, and is the preferred vinegar throughout Asia. Chinese brands are inexpensive and widely available, while the Japanese rice vinegar, used in sushi, is sweeter and milder.

Serves 4
Preparation time: **30 mins**
Cooking time: **10 mins**

First twist the heads off the lobsters.

Using pliers, twist off the undershell.

Index